All About Tomatoes

by Emma LaConti

Table of Contents

What Do You Know
About Tomatoes?...........2

Where Are
Tomatoes From?...........4

How Do You Grow
Tomatoes? 6

What Can You Make
with Tomatoes? 10

Comprehension Check.....16

What Do You Know About Tomatoes?

Tomatoes taste great. They are good for you, too! Tomatoes have a lot of vitamins.

↻ Tomatoes come in many different colors.

Not all tomatoes are red. They can be yellow, orange, pink, or white.

All tomatoes are green before they are ready to be picked. Then the tomatoes turn their true color. That's when they're ready to eat!

Tomatoes are ➲ brightest when they are ready to be picked.

Where Are Tomatoes From?

Tomatoes first grew in the Americas. The Aztecs and Incas grew them over 1,000 years ago.

⟲ Incas picked fruits and vegetables to trade in the early 1500s.

⋒ Tomatoes were sold in France
in the late 1500s.

Explorers took tomatoes home
to Europe. Many people thought
tomatoes would make them sick.
It was years before some people
would eat tomatoes.

How Do You Grow Tomatoes?

Tomatoes are fruits. They grow from seeds. They are easy to grow. Tomatoes need water, sunlight, and warmth. They won't grow in cold weather.

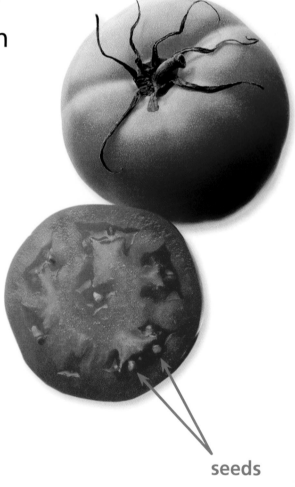

seeds

Tomatoes need good soil. They can grow in pots or in the ground.

↻ Plant seeds in good soil. Water them well. Soon plants will grow.

In four to six ➲ weeks, a plant might be this size.

As the plant grows, it gets taller. People may tie the prickly stem to a stick. Then the plant climbs up the stick.

Next is the blooming stage. Flowers appear. The flowers turn into fruit. Some kinds of tomatoes can be picked in about six more weeks.

⋔ A plant is tied to a stick.

⋔ Yellow flowers bloom.

⋔ Some plants grow up to six feet (1.8 meters) tall!

Some tomatoes are large. One kind of tomato can weigh as much as two pounds (I kilogram). You would need to use your muscles to lift a bag of them!

⬆ Tomatoes are different shapes and sizes. The small, round tomato on the left is called a cherry tomato.

What Can You Make with Tomatoes?

You can eat raw tomatoes. First, wash them. Then, cut them up for salads or sandwiches.

Tomato Sandwiches

Ingredients:
- Sliced bread or bagel
- Butter, cream cheese, or mayonnaise
- Sliced tomato
- Salt and pepper

1. Use a knife to spread butter, mayonnaise, or cream cheese on the bread.

2. Lay tomato slices on the bread.

3. Add a pinch each of salt and pepper.

4. You can cover this with another slice of bread.

Tomatoes can be cooked, too. They can be grilled, boiled, or even fried. Do you use ketchup? It is made from tomatoes.

⬆ Ketchup tastes good on some foods.

Grilled tomatoes ➲ are a tasty side dish.

Tomatoes don't have a scent. But they taste great in foods around the world.

Many dishes from India use tomatoes. Spaghetti sauce and pizza from Italy use them, too.

Pizza Margharita

Ingredients:

- **Pizza dough**
- **Chunky tomato sauce**
- **Grated fontina and romano cheese**
- **Olive oil**

1. Spread a thin layer of olive oil on the dough.

2. Add sauce and cheese on top.

3. Ask an adult to heat your pizza in the oven.

4. Wait for the cheese to melt. Then enjoy!

5: You can add a pinch of herbs (oregano or marjoram). Your pizza will have a spicy Italian taste and aroma.

Raw tomatoes are in Mexican salsa. Salsa is easy to make.

Salsa

See ingredients pictured below.

1. Have an adult chop tomatoes, chili peppers, onion, and cilantro.

2. Mix them together.

3. Add a little salt and sugar.

4. Eat salsa with tortilla chips.

 tomatoes

 chili peppers

 onion

 cilantro

Now you know all about tomatoes. People all over the world enjoy this tasty fruit.

⊙ This girl takes a bite out of a big tomato.

Tell your friends about tomatoes. Maybe they'll want to grow some to eat!

Comprehension Check

Retell

Use a Sequence Chart and the pictures to help you tell about this book.

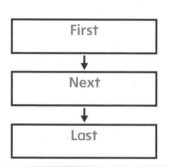

First
↓
Next
↓
Last

Think and Compare

1. Turn to page 10. What do you do before you add salt and pepper? What do you do after? *(Identify Sequence of Events)*

2. What fruit or vegetable have you seen growing? How was it the same or different from a tomato plant? *(Apply)*

3. Why do you think some people grow their own fruits and vegetables? *(Analyze)*